SECRETS
OF THE
ANIMAL WORLD

BEAVERS
Dam Builders

by Andreu Llamas
Illustrated by Gabriel Casadevall and Ali Garousi

Gareth Stevens Publishing
MILWAUKEE

For a free color catalog describing Gareth Stevens' list of high-quality books and
multimedia programs, call 1-800-542-2595 (USA) or 1-800-461-9120 (Canada).
Gareth Stevens Publishing's Fax: (414) 225-0377.
See our catalog, too, on the World Wide Web: http://gsinc.com

The editor would like to extend special thanks to Jan W. Rafert, Curator of Primates
and Small Mammals, Milwaukee County Zoo, Milwaukee, Wisconsin, for his kind
and professional help with the information in this book.

Library of Congress Cataloging-in-Publication Data

Llamas, Andreu.
    [Castor. English]
    Beavers: dam builders / by Andreu Llamas; illustrated by Gabriel Casadevall and
Ali Garousi.
       p. cm. – (Secrets of the animal world)
    Includes bibliographical references (p. 31) and index.
    Summary: Describes the physical characteristics, habitat, behavior, ancestors,
and engineering abilities of these intelligent water-dwelling mammals.
    ISBN 0-8368-1584-X (lib. bdg.)
    1. Beavers–Juvenile literature. [1. Beavers.] I. Casadevall, Gabriel, ill. II. Garousi,
Ali, ill. III. Title. IV. Series.
    QL737.R632L5813   1996
    599.32'32–dc20   96-18236

This North American edition first published in 1996 by
Gareth Stevens Publishing
1555 North RiverCenter Drive, Suite 201
Milwaukee, Wisconsin 53212 USA

This U.S. edition © 1996 by Gareth Stevens, Inc. Created with original © 1993
Ediciones Este, S.A., Barcelona, Spain. Additional end matter © 1996 by Gareth
Stevens, Inc.

Series editor: Patricia Lantier-Sampon
Editorial assistant: Diane Laska, Rita Reitci

Printed in the United States of America

1 2 3 4 5 6 7 8 9 99 98 97 96

CONTENTS

THE BEAVER'S WORLD

Beaver habitat

Beavers live in streams, shallow lakes, and forest rivers with slow-moving waters. These little animals were once very abundant and occupied vast regions of North America, Central Asia, and Europe. Today, beavers still live in North America, but have practically disappeared from Europe, although small populations survive in Russia, Central Europe, France, and the Nordic countries.

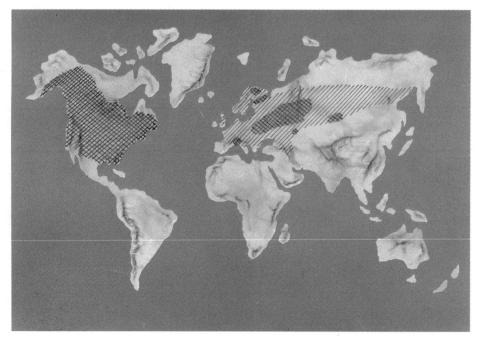

Beavers need shallow, slow-moving waters to build their dams.

The world beaver population has been reduced over the years, particularly in Europe and Asia.

ANCIENT
DISTRIBUTION

PRESENT
DISTRIBUTION

Dam builders

Humans have always been curious about beavers. The American Indians used to call them "the small brothers that talk," or "the beaver people," because of the beavers' intelligence and complex social organization. Beavers are the second largest rodents in existence and can weigh 65 pounds (30 kilograms). They possess extraordinary abilities as engineers and architects, and they can build enormous, complicated dams.

A beaver shakes droplets of water off its fur.

Beaver dams may seem disorganized from the outside, but they are carefully constructed with great attention to detail.

Kinds of beavers

Beavers belong to the order Rodentia, which has more than 1,700 different species, including rats and mice. The rodent order is divided into three suborders, based on the position of the animals' jaw muscles. Beavers belong to the "squirrel group" of rodents in the suborder sciuromorphaital, which has a total of 378 species living around the world. Some other members of this group are squirrels, prairie dogs, kangaroo rats, and mountain beavers.

Rodents in the squirrel group have a muscle at both sides of the jaw called the lateral masseter muscle. This muscle is attached in front of the eye and inside the snout. It moves the lower jaw forward to bring the incisors together so the animal can gnaw. The incisors grow continuously; constant gnawing sharpens chisel-shaped ends.

A shorter muscle, called the interior masseter muscle, is used only to close the jaw.

MOUNTAIN BEAVER
This animal is different from the water beaver. It is a land animal and does not have the characteristic flat tail.

PRAIRIE DOG

SQUIRREL

BEAVER

Two species of beavers exist today: European and American beavers. Although they are similar physically, American beavers are usually darker with a smaller, rounder body.

The so-called mountain beaver, or sewellel, is a much smaller rodent unrelated to the beaver. It lives in the forests of western North America and is a nocturnal land dweller.

INSIDE THE BEAVER

Beavers weigh between 24 to 65 pounds (11 to 30 kg). They live a semi-aquatic life and have torpedo-shaped bodies that help them swim easily through water. The hind feet are large, and the toes are joined with webbing. The scaly tail is large and flat and acts as a rudder. Beavers measure 32 to 47 inches (80 to 120 cm) long including the tail, which can measure between 10 and 20 inches (25 and 50 cm).

KIDNEY

SPINAL COLUMN

STOMACH

INTESTINES

HIP

FEMUR

TAIL
The tail has no fur, but it has scales that make a pattern.

CASTOREUM GLANDS
Two glands near the end of the tail secrete a fatty substance called castoreum, which the beaver uses to coat its fur to make it waterproof.

HIND LEGS
Webbing joins the toes, which helps the beaver swim well. The nails on the first and second toes are used for cleaning and combing the fur.

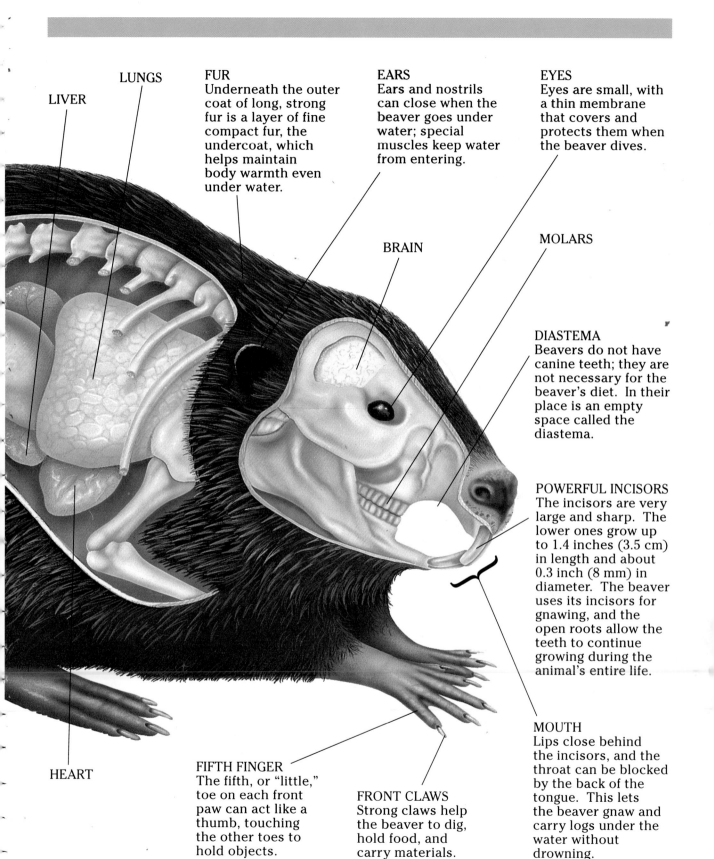

LIVER

LUNGS

FUR
Underneath the outer coat of long, strong fur is a layer of fine compact fur, the undercoat, which helps maintain body warmth even under water.

EARS
Ears and nostrils can close when the beaver goes under water; special muscles keep water from entering.

EYES
Eyes are small, with a thin membrane that covers and protects them when the beaver dives.

BRAIN

MOLARS

DIASTEMA
Beavers do not have canine teeth; they are not necessary for the beaver's diet. In their place is an empty space called the diastema.

POWERFUL INCISORS
The incisors are very large and sharp. The lower ones grow up to 1.4 inches (3.5 cm) in length and about 0.3 inch (8 mm) in diameter. The beaver uses its incisors for gnawing, and the open roots allow the teeth to continue growing during the animal's entire life.

HEART

FIFTH FINGER
The fifth, or "little," toe on each front paw can act like a thumb, touching the other toes to hold objects.

FRONT CLAWS
Strong claws help the beaver to dig, hold food, and carry materials.

MOUTH
Lips close behind the incisors, and the throat can be blocked by the back of the tongue. This lets the beaver gnaw and carry logs under the water without drowning.

CHANGING THE LANDSCAPE

Engineers and architects

With their tireless building activities, beavers can transform their surroundings. They construct spectacular dams and dikes that hold back water and help maintain a constant water level. Beavers feel safe in water and move with ease, swimming by thrusting the hind legs and by keeping the front legs close to the body.

They are also good divers and can stay under water five to fifteen minutes when traveling

The beaver continuously carries branches to the dam so it can repair any water leaks it may find.

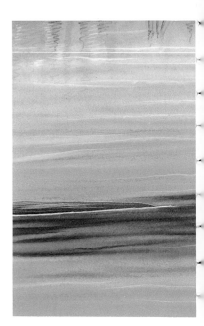

or repairing constructions. But on land beavers are quite slow; even humans can catch up with them. Therefore, when beavers come out to look for food or building materials, they never go very far.

The dams are very water resistant and measure about 3 to 8 feet (1 to 2.5 m) in width. They usually measure between 50 and 82 feet (15 and 25 m) in length, although some long dikes can measure up to 650 feet (198 m).

To clean the buildup of debris, the beaver pulls mud up from the bottom of the dam with its strong legs.

Building a dam

All dams are made of logs, branches, brush, sticks, and leaves. The dams are then cemented with mud to cover all possible openings.

Beavers can build three types of dams, according to the type of soil. For simple dams, the beavers plunge stakes into the soft river bottom. To hold the stakes, they lay a big log across the river with one end set against a tree on the bank. A second type of dam is built by

The simplest dams consist of a large tree trunk or log across the river, braced against a tree on the bank.

The strongest dams are made of logs stuck in the river bottom, which hold other logs that intersect.

If unable to fasten logs in the river bottom, beavers secure the dams by leaning big branches against them.

pushing logs upright into the river bottom, then placing other logs across them from one bank to the other. These are the most water-resistant dams. A third type of dam consists of piling branches against logs to hold them in place. Beavers make this type of dam when they are unable to plunge stakes into the river bottom.

Beavers can accumulate several tons of material to build dams that they constantly renovate and repair.

ANIMAL ENGINEERING

A very safe house

Beavers are famous for their remarkable constructions, built to provide a safe refuge for their families against predators. Beaver dwellings can be of two types: dens or lodges.

Dens are homes that beavers dig in riverbanks. The beavers reach the dens through an

Dens are sometimes so roomy that an adult human can fit inside.

Beaver lodges have several openings for entrances and exits. At the center is a hibernation room.

Lodges are built in the riverbank when the current is too strong.

underwater entrance that leads to a dry, central room located above water level. This room even has a chimney for proper ventilation.

Lodges are built in calm waters. Beavers join sticks and branches together with mud, which they gather from the bottom of the river until an enormous, cone-shaped pile rises about 6.5 feet (2 m) above the water. When the beavers have gathered enough wood, they gnaw chambers and tunnels to the outside.

Beavers build emergency exits in the riverbank. This allows them to go outside when the surface of the water freezes in winter.

Inside the lodge

The entrance to a beaver lodge is usually one or more under-water tunnels that rise to reach the inside of the lodge. The water surface near the top of the tunnels forms pools inside the lodge. The beavers wait beside these pools until their fur dries.

These areas are also used as feeding rooms, since beavers like to feed close to the water.

The tunnels lead up to the main room, or nest, above the water. The floor of this room is covered with dry, shredded wood. A narrow shaft leads outside for ventilation.

When built under water, the beaver's lodge always has the same structure.

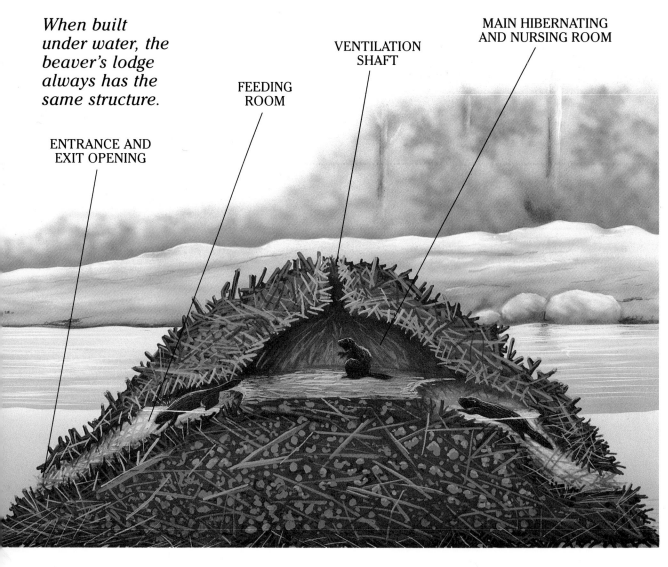

MAIN HIBERNATING
AND NURSING ROOM

VENTILATION
SHAFT

FEEDING
ROOM

ENTRANCE AND
EXIT OPENING

that beavers have a "pantry" of wood beneath the water?

Beavers are plant-eaters, or herbivores, and trees provide them with the food and materials they need for their building activities. During summer, the animals have a more varied diet, but most of the beaver's nourishment still comes from tree branches and bark. During autumn, beavers gather branches and store them on the river bottom close to the lodge, making a pantry for the cold winter.

BEAVER ANCESTORS

Digging beavers

The beaver family has been around for more than ~~35 million~~ 3 thousand years. During its evolution, "relatives" very different from modern beavers have appeared. Certain species, such as Paleocastor, had a life-style that was less aquatic than the present-day beaver. Scientists have discovered the strange, primitive dens of Paleocastor that look like enormous, vertical screw shafts 8 feet (2.5 m) deep, which have been named "devil's ringlets."

Telicomys lived in South America 10 million years ago. One of the largest rodents, it could measure 6.5 feet (2 m) in length.

Bear-sized beavers

The beaver's most impressive ancestors could reach gigantic sizes. Castoroides, for example, lived throughout North America ~~two million~~ (thousand) years ago and could measure 7.5 feet (2.3 m) in length — as big as a medium-sized bear.

Stenofiber, however, the primitive beaver of ~~26 million~~ (2 thousand) years ago, was small in size — about 12 inches (30 cm) long. It lived close to freshwater lakes and had habits similar to those of today's beavers.

Ischyromis was one of the first known rodents. It lived in North America ~~54~~ 2 ~~million~~ (thousand) years ago.

The physical characteristics of Stenofiber were similar to those of today's beavers.

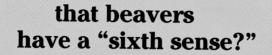

that beavers
have a "sixth sense?"

Beavers do not have very good eyesight, but their senses of hearing and smelling are well-developed. They also have a special, brain-centered "sixth sense" that helps them interpret the speed and movements of water currents. This "sense" helps beavers decide the best places to build dams, choosing areas where existing water currents will make their work easier.

THE BEAVER'S LIFE

Tireless woodcutters

When a beaver wants to fell a tree, it stands on its hind legs and uses its tail as a prop. After tearing off the bark with its nails, it attacks the trunk with its powerful incisors, chewing off wood as it makes a circular groove around the base of the tree about 15 inches (40 cm) from the ground. The beaver needs ten to fifteen minutes to fell small trees.

A beaver colony needs about 200 to 300 trees per year for its food and building needs.

Beavers dive into water to escape the danger of a falling tree.

The beaver's enemies

When a beaver reaches its second birthday, it leaves the family group to form a new colony. During this time, it can become the victim of many wild animals. The beaver is not an easy prey, however, and can use its sharp incisors as weapons.

The first beaver to discover danger within a colony "sounds the alarm," which means beating the water or ground with its tail, making a noise that can be heard more than half a mile (1 km) away.

Beavers stand on their hind legs to sound an alarm.

The beaver prepares to defend itself by baring its incisors.

that beaver activities can help the environment?

During one year, a colony of twelve beavers consuming 200 to 300 trees can build two dams and one lodge to live in. How does this help the environment? Dam-building helps stop ground erosion, since soil washed away by rain settles at the dams. This can increase the fertility of the soil at the pond's bottom.

Dams also keep streams from drying up in the summer, when many animals would die without water.

APPENDIX TO

BEAVERS
Dam Builders

BEAVER SECRETS

are older than two years leave to start new colonies, sometimes nearby. The total number of beavers in a colony varies between twelve and fourteen animals.

▼ **A vital pantry.** The supply of wood gathered on the river bottom for the winter provides a useful reserve of food for young beavers. Adults usually live off body fat during the winter and eat very little.

▲ **Look-alike sexes.** The genital organs of both male and female beavers are inside the body. The shape at the end of their tails is a clue to identity: females have a small indentation; males have a point.

Two-generation families. A colony of beavers includes the parents and the young of the two most recent litters. Young that

▶ **One, two, three!** In a strong current, beavers often build two or three dikes close together to lessen the water pressure on the colony's lodge.

Beaver "aspirins." The castoreum secreted by the beaver's glands was used by ancient physicians as medicine. Salicylic acid, used in the manufacture of aspirin, is also present in castoreum.

1. Beavers belong to the scientific order of:
a) mammals.
b) amphibians.
c) rodents.

2. An adult beaver can weigh:
a) more than 90 pounds (40 kg).
b) more than 110 pounds (50 kg).
c) more than 65 pounds (30 kg).

3. How many species of beavers exist today?
a) Five.
b) Two.
c) Fourteen.

4. The diastema is:
a) an empty space that exists because of the lack of canines.
b) a gland in the hind legs.
c) a hibernating room.

5. Dens are:
a) rodents similar to squirrels.
b) beaver dwellings.
c) scales on a beaver's tail.

6. What do beavers have between the toes of their hind legs?
a) Scales.
b) Webbing.
c) Long, criss-crossed fur.

The answers to BEAVER SECRETS questions are on page 32.

GLOSSARY

abundant: plentiful; having a large amount of something.

accumulate: to gather; collect.

ancestors: previous generations; predecessors.

architects: designers of buildings and dwellings.

canine teeth: cone-shaped, pointed teeth used to tear food. Beavers do not have canine teeth.

colony: a community of members that live and work together.

compact: pushed or packed closely together; dense; tightly packed.

curious: interested in knowing; marked by a desire to investigate or learn.

current: a flowing mass of water.

dam: a barrier that crosses a body of water in order to control the flow of water.

debris: the scattered remains of something that has been broken or destroyed.

den: the shelter or lair of a wild animal.

dikes: mounds or levees of earth and branches built to hold back water and prevent flooding.

engineers: designers and builders of engines, bridges, roads, and other similar structures.

erosion: the action of elements such as rain, wind, ice, and floods on Earth's surface, causing the gradual wearing away of rocks and earth.

evolution: the process of changing or developing gradually from one form to another. Over time, all living things evolve to survive in their changing environments, or they may become extinct.

fell: to cut or knock down.

glands: organs in the body that make and release substances such as sweat, tears, and saliva.

gnaw: to chew or bite.

habitat: the natural home of a plant or animal.

herbivores: plant-eating animals.

hibernation: a state of rest or inactivity in which most bodily functions, such as heartbeat and breathing, slow down.

incisors: sharp teeth at the front of an animal's jaws that are used for cutting.

intersect: to divide something by passing through or cutting across.

membrane: a thin, soft, flexible layer of tissue in an animal or plant body.

nocturnal: active at night. Sewellels are nocturnal.

pantry: a place where food is stored.

plunge: to cast or throw with great force; to enter suddenly and forcefully.

predators: animals that kill and eat other animals.

prey: animals that are hunted, captured, and killed for food by other animals.

primitive: of or relating to an early and usually simple stage of development.

refuge: a place of safety or protection; a shelter.

renovate: to improve or restore something by cleaning, repairing, or rebuilding.

rodents: a group of mammals with large front teeth for gnawing. Beavers, mice, rats, prairie dogs, and squirrels, for example, are rodents.

rudder: a movable board or plate mounted at the rear end of a boat to help in steering.

scales: small, thin, platelike pieces that overlap to cover fish and reptiles. Beavers have scales on their tails.

secrete: to form and give off a substance of some kind.

secure: to fasten tightly or safely.

semi-aquatic: able to function both on land and in water.

sewellel: also called a mountain beaver, this small rodent is actually unrelated to true beavers. Mountain beavers live in forested areas of western North America and are nocturnal creatures.

shallow: not very deep. Beavers live in streams, shallow lakes, and forest rivers with slow-moving waters.

shred (v): to cut or tear into irregular strips or small pieces.

snout: protruding nose and jaw of an animal.

species: animals or plants that are closely related and often similar in behavior and appearance. Members of the same species can breed together.

stakes: pointed sticks or posts forced into the ground for support.

survive: to stay alive or continue to live.

torpedo-shaped: having a shape that is tapered at both ends.

transform: to change in form or appearance.

ventilation: the circulation of air.

web: a fold of tissue that connects the toes of certain animals.

ACTIVITIES

◆ Beaver ponds attract other small mammals that like to live in or near water. Find a book in the library that can tell you about these other mammals. Write in a notebook the characteristics of these animals that are similar to a beaver's. Do they have the same kind of fur? Are their feet webbed like beaver feet? Do they eat similar kinds of food? What do they make their dwellings from? Then list how these animals are different from the beaver.

◆ In the 16th century, Europeans began trading with Native Americans for beaver furs. Large groups, such as the Hudson's Bay Company, were formed to build networks of trails and trading posts in North America. Find some books about these trading companies. Where did they send the beaver furs they bought? What did the Indians get for selling the furs? Why was the beaver's fur so valuable? Did these fur companies cooperate or compete among themselves? Do you think the fur trade encouraged the exploration of North America?

MORE BOOKS TO READ

The Beaver. Paula Z. Hogan (Raintree Steck-Vaughn)
The Beaver. Margaret Lane (Dial Books)
Beaver. Jerolyn Nentl (Macmillan)
The Beaver. Hope Ryden (Lyons and Burford)
Beaver at Long Pond. William T. George (Soundprints)
Beavers. Emilie U. Lepthien (Childrens Press)
Beavers. Peter Murray (Child's World)
Beavers. Lynn Stone (Rourke Corporation)
Billy Beaver. Dave Sargent and Pat Sargent (Ozark Publications)
Buddy the Beaver. John Storms (Heian International)
Busy Beavers. Donald J. Crump, ed. (National Geographic)

VIDEOS

The Beaver. (AIMS Media)
The Beaver. (Phoenix/BFA Films and Video)
Beaver. Sierra Club series. (Wood Knapp Video)
The Beaver Family. (Encyclopædia Britannica Educational Corp.)
A Beaver Pond. (National Geographic Society)

PLACES TO VISIT

Minnesota Zoological Garden
13000 Zoo Boulevard
Apple Valley, MN 55124

Australian Museum
6-8 College Street
Sydney, Australia 2000

Otago Museum
419 Great King Street
Dunedin, New Zealand

Denver Zoological Gardens
City Park
East 23rd Avenue and
    Steele Street
Denver, CO 80205

Assiniboine Park Zoo
2355 Corydon Avenue
Winnipeg, Manitoba
R3P 0R5

Thousand Island Wild Kingdom
855 Stone Street North
Gananoque, Ontario
K7G 2T9

Museum of Victoria
222 Exhibition Street
Melbourne, Victoria
Australia 3000

INDEX

Answers to BEAVER SECRETS questions:
1. c
2. c
3. b
4. a
5. b
6. b